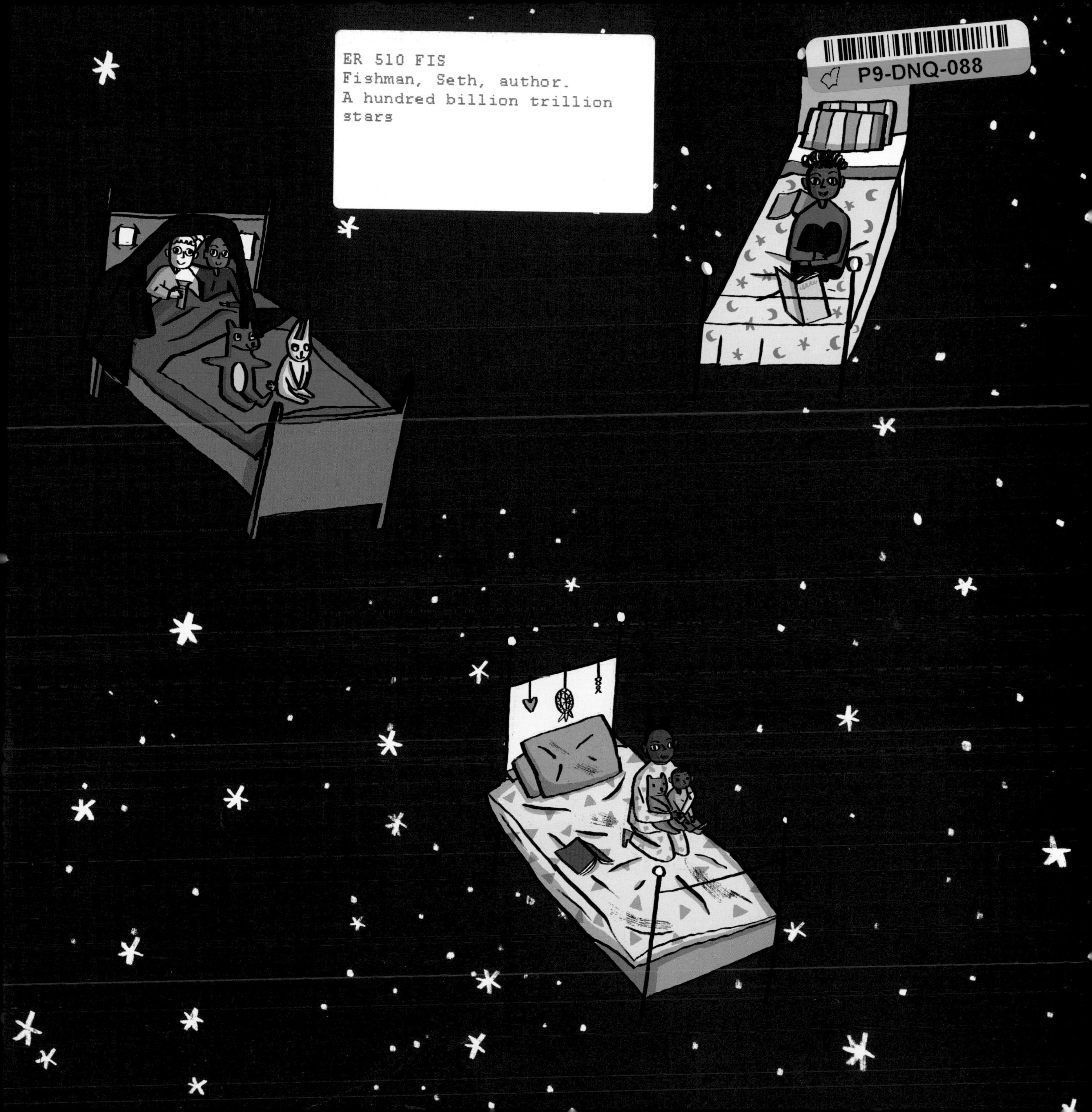

For Wes, up above the world so high—S. F.

A Hundred Billion Trillion Stars
Text copyright © 2017 by Seth Fishman
Illustrations copyright © 2017 by Isabel Greenberg
All rights reserved. Manufactured in China.
For information address HarperCollins Children's Books,
a division of HarperCollins Publishers,
195 Broadway, New York, NY 10007.
www.harpercollinschildrens.com

The full-color art was prepared digitally.
The text type is 20-point Abadi MT.

Library of Congress Cataloging-in-Publication Data

Names: Fishman, Seth, author. | Greenberg, Isabel,
illustrators.
Title: A hundred billion trillion stars / by Seth Fishman ;
illustrated by Isabel Greenberg.
Description: First edition. | New York, NY : Greenwillow
Books, an imprint of HarperCollinsPublishers, [2017]. |
Audience: Ages 4-8. | Audience: K to grade 3.
Identifiers: LCCN 2016037807 |
ISBN 9780062455789 (hardcover)
Subjects: LCSH: Mathematics—Miscellanea—
Juvenile literature. | Cardinal numbers—Miscellanea—
Juvenile literature.
Classification: LCC QA40.5 .F575 2017 | DDC 510.2—dc23
LC record available at https://lccn.loc.gov/2016037807

19 20 21 SCP 10 9 8
First Edition

GREENWILLOW BOOKS

A HUNDRED BILLION TRILLION STARS

BY Seth Fishman

ILLUSTRATED BY Isabel Greenberg

Greenwillow Books
An Imprint of HarperCollinsPublishers

Let me tell you a secret.

The sun is just a star.

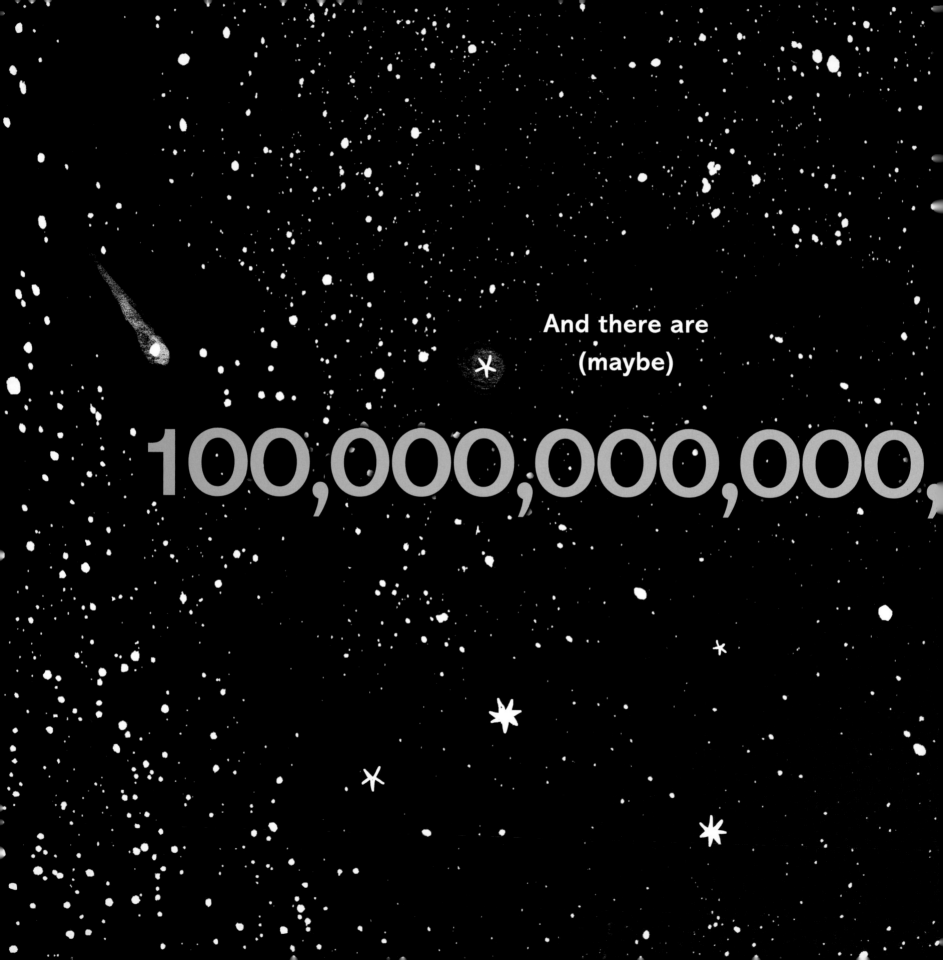

And there are
(maybe)

100,000,000,000,

000,000,000,000 stars.

a hundred billion trillion

Circling around our star is a planet
that is blue and green.

Us

Blue because it's covered by
370,000,000,000,000,000,000
gallons of water.

three hundred seventy billion billion

Green because it's covered in
3,000,000,000,000
trees.

three trillion

On the other side of the planet,
where the sun isn't shining,
you can see bright lights
like little stars all over its surface.

Those are the lights that come from
2,500,000 cities and towns and villages
filled with people . . . .

two million five hundred thousand

some even reading books.

JUST. LIKE. YOU.

7,500,000,000 people live in those cities and on that planet.
But do you want to know another secret?

So do 10,000,000,000,000,000 ants.
The strange thing is that seven billion five hundred million
humans weigh about the same as ten quadrillion ants.

Which is still only a
small fraction—or portion—of the
13,000,000,000,000,000,000,000,000
pounds the planet itself weighs.

thirteen million billion billion

That's heavy enough to make a big dip in space
and pull the moon into orbit, where it circles and circles the earth,
240,000 miles away.

two hundred forty thousand

This dip is a force called gravity.
Gravity is also what pulls you back to the ground
when you try to jump to the moon.

240,000 miles is about
ten times around the earth,
or almost 420,000,000 yous

four hundred twenty million

(or dogs or smallish snakes
or guitars or baseball bats)
lined up head to foot.

Now take a deep breath
and hold it for five seconds.

Just do that another
6,307,200 times,
and you'll be a year older!

six million three hundred
seven thousand two hundred

Or don't. You'll be a year older in 31,536,000 seconds anyway.

thirty-one million five hundred thirty-six thousand

This entire world is filled with crazy numbers,
built one on top of the other,
making it whole and complete.

There are about
1,620 trillion raindrops
in an average thunderstorm.

The highest wave ever
surfed was as tall as a
ten-story building.

The average person walks
something like 100,000 miles
in their lifetime,
or five times around the world.

A great white shark has about 300 teeth.
(You have twenty, but will have thirty-two
when you get older.)

Only 546 people have been in space.
The longest a person has spent
in space at one time is 437 days.

There are probably at least
37 billion rabbits in the world.

In the course of an average
lifetime, you might eat up
to 70 pounds of bugs . . .
or more.

The tallest building
in the world is
2,722 feet tall.
It is in Dubai.

By the time you're done reading this book,
almost every single number in it will have changed,
getting bigger or smaller
right before your eyes.

Even the number of stars.

BLAST OFF!

I can
tell you
one more

SECRET

about something you can find somewhere among the

100,000,000,000,000,000,000,000

stars.

There's only one of YOU.

Right here,

right now,

reading
this book.

Author's Note

I think I owe you an explanation. I'm sure you're wondering how in the (wide) world I know the number of stars, or ants, or raindrops. I definitely didn't pull out a telescope, look up into the night sky, and begin counting. If I did that, I would spend my entire life at that telescope and would never come close to finishing.

Instead, I discovered them through scientific articles, and math, and very intelligent guesswork, and the help of a genius I know named Randall Munroe.

These numbers are sort-of-definitely-ALMOST true. Let me explain. Some of these numbers change so quickly that to give you an exact number would be impossible. For instance, we don't really know if the full weight of all the ants on earth equals the full weight of humans. But we can estimate that there are 3.5 million ants per acre in the Amazon rain forest. With some serious snooping, fact-checking, and extrapolating we can estimate a very large number of ants on earth, one that means the combined weight of all these ants should be *near* the combined weight of all humans, or maybe dogs, or mice. And yes, you might eat some of those ants. You might eat many different types of bugs—though of course I don't know exactly how many, or whether you'll do it on purpose. Maybe a fly will zip into your mouth as you bike, or you'll swallow a spider while you snore at night. But it will be *near* 70 pounds' worth over the course of your life (about the total weight of a golden retriever).

Estimates can help you imagine sizes and compare one big fact to another. That is why this book is called *A Hundred Billion Trillion Stars*, and not *One Hundred Nineteen Sextillion Fifty-Seven Quintillion Seven Hundred Thirty-Seven Quadrillion One Hundred Eighty-Three Trillion Four Hundred Sixty-Two Billion Three Hundred Seven Million Four Hundred Ninety-One Thousand Six Hundred Nine Stars*. We can get very near the correct number on many things, near enough for us to understand how big they are—especially in comparison to the world around us.

Here's what's really important: these huge numbers are around us *everywhere*. They're in atoms and ants and stars, linking everything together. You have the exact same thing that stars are made of inside of you. And the sun, just a star, has some of you in it, too. So the next time you're staring at the night sky, don't bother counting the stars, just watch them all shine.

billion
trillion
(or sextillion)   quadrillion   billion   thousand

100,000,000,000,000,000,000,000

billion   trillion   million   hundred
billion
(or quintillion)